Ordo Angelorum
Society

Dedicated to

Saint Michael and the Nine Choirs of Angels. May they watch over us and protect us now and always.

September 29, Feast of Saint Michael the Archangel

Contents

History of the Saint Michael Prayer and Exorcism

In 1884, Pope Leo XIII was given a vision during mass. He heard a conversation between God and Satan. The conversation was reminiscent of Job. Satan was given 100 years in which to attack the Church, and Satan chose the twentieth century. The pope immediately sat down and composed an exorcism prayer directed to Saint Michael.

Ordo Angelorum, or Order of the Angels, gives glory to God for his most sublime creation and the mystical perfection of their nine choirs and hierarchy.

God's Coming Justice

As the world is spiralling into sin and the enemy appears to be gaining more victories each day, faithful Catholics are sensing the impending chastisement mentioned in the 8th chapter of the Apocalypse which directly follows the protection of the elect by the angels. The angels carry out God's mercy and then they carry out God's justice.

The Efficacy of Our Prayers

Through the prayers of the faithful, that the number of the elect may increase to the fullest measure, and these elect may be spared the coming chastisement. Padre Pio, the famous priest who had the visible wounds of Christ in his own body and died right before the Great Apostasy in 1968, urged the frequent recitation of the prayer, "O Jesus, save the elect in the hour of darkness."

Strike the Shepherd

Clearly, Pope Leo was told much more than is related in the story, as the prayer that he composed specifically states that the Shepherd (Pope) will be struck and the sheep (Faithful Catholics) will scatter (see below). This is a direct quote from Our Lord in reference to Peter's abandonment and denial. This would not necessarily refer to a martyred Pope, as for 1800 years before this vision, dozens of Popes have been martyred or murdered. In all these cases, the sheep were not dispersed. No, this act of "striking" must be apocalyptic in nature to generate this vision, and the subsequent apostasy that we now experience. Since this vision concerns the dramatic dispersal of the Faithful, it could only refer to the Second Vatican Council and the creation of the Anti-church of the New Order.

During the Middle Ages, excommunication was also styled as "drawing the sword of St. Peter" and in dogmatic documents (as in the Fourth Lateran Council), we see the phrase "struck with the sword of excommunication." The vision could more probably apply to a true Vicar of Christ who teaches heresy and loses his office. This fallen Pope would do much harm to the Church and be responsible for the scattered flock we see today. Angelo Roncali, aka Antipope John XXIII was a known Freemason and therefore ineligible even to become Pope in the first place, as was Montini, aka Antipope Paul VI. After Paul, those falsely occupying the chair of Peter were professed leaders of a non-Catholic sect and not to be confused at all with Popes of the Catholic Church.

There are two possibilities for who this stricken Vicar could be. The first is Pope Pius XII, as he is responsible for any number of errors. These errors are enumerated in Bishop Sandborn's letter (nearly all of which happened after the allocution to the midwives which appeared to contradict the dogmatic decrees on marriage, Casti Connubii and also contradict decrees on Salvation):
"Sixty Years Since the Death of Pope Pius XII" https://inveritateblog.com/2018/10/29/sixty-years-since-the-death-of-pius-xii/

The other possibility for this "striking of excommunication" may have been Cardinal Siri, if he were indeed elected Pope at the conclave of 1958. There is quite a lot of evidence to this effect, but Siri never came out publicly that he had been elected and was reported to have said the mass of the New Order. Either or both of the above scenarios was enough to create the destruction and scattering of sheep that we see today. The next True Vicar of Christ (may he come quickly) will have to settle this once and for all.

The history of the events leading up to the creation of the Church of the New Order is well depicted in the video The 3rd Secret of Fatima, 3rd Edition which is produced by Most Holy Family Monastery https://www.youtube.com/watch?v=VB_hUdRKi4o

There is evidence that the scattered sheep have begun to find their way back to the Lord's pasture. The best explanation of why they were scattered, and how they are to return can be found at gatheredsheep.org, or in the book of that same name on Amazon, written by C.D.M, OSF

Who Are These Elect?

We can look to the Prophet Ezekial for clues as to who these people with this blessed mark shall be, and what will determine who receives this life-saving sign from the angels.

> *"And the Lord said to him: Go through the midst of the city, through the midst of Jerusalem: and mark Thau upon the foreheads of the men that sigh, and mourn for all the abominations that are committed in the midst thereof. 5And to the others he said in my hearing: Go ye after him through the city, and strike: let not your eyes spare, nor be ye moved with pity. 6Utterly destroy old and young, maidens, children and women: but upon whomsoever you shall see Thau, kill him not, and begin ye at my sanctuary."*

The letter Thau is the same as our lowercase T. It is, in fact, the cross. Thus, in our day, those who weep and morn over the abominations occurring in the New Israel, which is Rome and the Vatican would be those worthy of the blessed mark. But this symbol of Thau goes even further. When considering that the Pope had this vision during mass, it is then appropriate that we should find clues to this prophecy within the mass itself. To this end, we can see a rather significant reference to the Thau in the Te Igitur. We read in the Saint Andrew Daily Missal:

"The letter T commencing the prayer Te Igitur was usually adorned with a figure of the Christ because it has the form of a cross. Later this was made into a picture of Calvary, to remind us that the sacrifice of mass is the renewal of that of the Cross."

The Te Igitur is the most controversial section of the Traditional Latin Mass today, for it is here where the priest implores God the Father to accept this sacrifice and to apply its saving graces to the Catholic faithful, united to the Pope and Bishops. It is controversial as there are many priests who call themselves Catholic, yet who persist in the pernicious heresy of uniting themselves, their sacrifice, and the faithful, to the manifest heretic Bergoglio i.e., Antipope Francis. It is to this very subject, of the empty papacy, which concerns the original long-form Saint Michael prayer, "In the Holy Place itself, where has been set up the See of the most blessed Peter and the Chair of Truth for the light of the world, they have raised the throne of their abominable impiety, with the iniquitous design that when the Pastor has been struck, the sheep may be scattered."

We see in this passage of the prayer, that not only has the Pastor been struck, but that the evil doers have also set up their own throne, to wit, an anti-Church and anti-Pope. Considering that this vacant papacy has come to pass since the sect of the New Order (Vatican II), and the open abominations which have been carried out not only by Anti-pope Francis, but by his damnable precursors, no one with good will should be deceived any longer.

The Truth is plain, and as plain as the necessity of Supernatural Faith for salvation. Anyone with an average intellectual capability, who persists in recognizing as valid the sect of the New Order, and its putrid hierarchy, is in serious danger of not receiving this Mark of Grace and Protection. In other words, the "Recognize and Resist" stance is on very shaky theological ground, and those who persist in this delusion run the risk of losing the help of the angles, and even losing their souls. As Scripture also tells us concerning this wicked and false church, "And I heard another voice from heaven, saying: Go out from her, my people; that you be not partakers of her sins, and that you receive not of her plagues."

The clerics of the SSPX, and other groups like them, are like the Rich Man, who although have "kept the commandments all of their lives", refuse to leave the riches of their father (Archbishop LeFebvre) and follow Our Lord into poverty. Remember friends, that, just like the Rich Man, Our Lord loves you and wants you to save your souls. Your conscience has been bothering you for years, if you stay separated from the true Church, you shall perish. Come, follow Him, and be free.

Te Igitur in the Latin Altar Missal

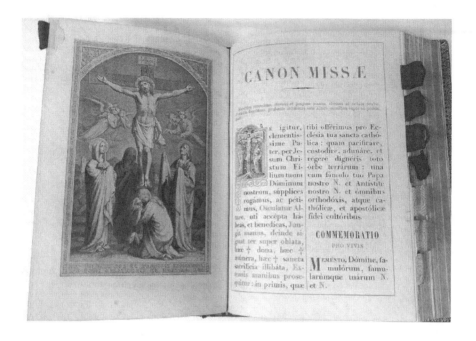

Additionally, we must consider the specific language of the section of the Mass following the Te Igitur, where the celebrant unites himself with a true Pontiff. He doesn't say, "I unite myself with", or "I wish to be in union with", or any number of ways to get this point across. God in His Providence has the priest say, "Una cum (one with) our Pontiff, (add name)." The use of the phrase "one with" is unique to this sacrament. Again, nothing is a coincidence, and this phrase is found rather conspicuously and germanely in an admonition from Saint Paul in Ist Corinthians, Chapter 6:

> "Know you not that your bodies are the members of Christ ? Shall I then take the members of Christ, and make them the members of an harlot ? God forbid. Or know you not, that he who is joined to a harlot, is made *one body*"

Considering that apostasy is spiritual adultery, and that the New Order Church is portrayed in the Apocalypse as a harlot sitting on seven hills, drinking the wine of her fornication, it should come as a surprise to no one that God would consider joining oneself to the leader of this apostate sect as adultery.

Along with the spiritual adultery, the followers of the "recognize and resist" position (that the leaders or "Popes" of the Novus Ordo sect are simultaneously the leaders of the Catholic Church) have painted themselves into a schismatic corner. To openly disobey a true Vicar of Christ, set up a parallel hierarchy (bishops and priests) in opposition to his Church and then to be excommunicated by him directly, is the literal definition of schism. Anyone with goodwill and even a tiny bit of common sense must admit this. The Sede-vacantist, on the other hand, are operating under the legal precept of Epikeia to consecrate bishops without papal permission. This is, in the absence of a Pope, the salvation of souls is the highest law of the Church. The use of this concept in law cannot apply when there is a valid Roman Pontiff.

In 1988, Archbishop Lefebvre and Bishop Castro de Mayer of Brazil, consecrated four SSPX priests to be bishops against the direct will of Antipope John Paul II. It is well known that Bishop Castro de Mayer was an outspoken Sede-vacantist. He was even walking around the room of the consecration proclaiming, "We have no pope." For Castro de Mayer, the brave act of consecrating in the absence of a Roman Pontiff was done out of necessity in the greatest time of peril the Church has known. On the other hand, for LeFebvre, who openly recognized John Paul II as a valid Catholic Pontiff, his action was a public act of schism. We do not have to guess or even assume what LeFebvre was thinking, as he told us himself right before the consecrations:

> .. this ceremony, which is apparently done against the will of Rome, is in no way a schism. We are not schismatics! If an excommunication was pronounced against the bishops of China, who separated themselves from Rome and put themselves under the Chinese government, one very easily understands why Pope Pius XII

excommunicated them. There is no question of us separating ourselves from Rome, nor of putting ourselves under a foreign government, nor of establishing a sort of parallel church as the Bishops of Palmar de Troya have done in Spain. They have even elected a pope, formed a college of cardinals... It is out of the question for us to do such things. Far from us be this miserable thought to separate ourselves from Rome.¹

LeFebvre, fully admits that he regards "the will of Rome" to be the ultimate authority, and thus admits that he is going against the will of the person he considers to be the Roman Pontiff. In true Modernist fashion, he says one thing and does just the opposite. The conservative laity may hear what they want to hear, but Rome saw through the contradiction. Two days later, On 2 July, Anti-Pope John Paul II condemned the consecration and "excommunicated" LeFebvre in his apostolic letter Ecclesia Dei,

> *In itself, this act was one of disobedience to the Roman Pontiff in a very grave matter and of supreme importance for the unity of the church, such as is the ordination of bishops whereby the apostolic succession is sacramentally perpetuated. Hence such disobedience – which implies in practice the*

*rejection of the Roman primacy – constitutes a
schismatic act. In performing such an act,
notwithstanding the formal canonical warning
sent to them by the Cardinal Prefect of the
Congregation for Bishops on 17 June last,
Mons. Lefebvre and the priests Bernard
Fellay, Bernard Tissier de Mallerais, Richard
Williamson and Alfonso de Galarreta, have
incurred the grave penalty of
excommunication envisaged by ecclesiastical
law*

And thus, Archbishop LeFebvre became the victim of
his own vacillating position. On the contrary, Bishop Castro
de Mayer had nothing to fear from an empty papal chair, a
chair which remains vacant to this day. The truth is that one
can't be excommunicated from the Catholic Church by the
leader of a non-Catholic sect. The "Nopes" of the Sect of
the New Ordo have no more power over faithful Catholics
than the Anglican Archbishop of Canterbury or the
Orthodox Patriarch of Constantinople.

Sede-vacantists function out of necessity in preserving
the sacraments in the *absence of a true pontiff,* not in
opposition to one. Any of the Sede clergy would submit to a
true Pontiff whenever God should will to provide one.
Indeed, they pray for that daily. In the 1970s and 1980s,
the newly ordained Sede-vacantist priests united into one
body with the remnant of the faithful existing clergy who
held fast to the Catholic Traditions. This remnant has all

but passed on, but their spiritual sons carry on their mission.

Each time I have approached an SSPX priest on this issue (I have quite literally backed a few into a corner until they would give me an answer), they all focus on three points. They say:

> 1. We are following the position of Archbishop Lefebvre.
> 2. If Francis (JP II, Benedict, etc.) is not the pope of the Catholic Church, and the Cardinals are not Cardinals of the Catholic Church, then there is no way for us to have a True Pope again.
> 3. "Pope" (fill in the blank), may be a bad Catholic, but he is still our Father. And one's father doesn't stop being a father just because he is bad.

The obvious answer to the first response is that the archbishop lived in a time of confusion, when there was no Internet to really see clearly what was going on. But, even without the Internet, he most assuredly had enough information just from Paul VI's new sacraments which were an obvious act of apostasy to any educated Catholic. Next came the Assisi debacle (John Paul II's horrendous monstrosity of false ecumenism-see John Paul the Great...Apostate! Wojtyla's Assisi 1986 in Novus Ordo Watch).

There is ample proof that the archbishop himself was Sede-vacantist. Father Anthony Cekada, who knew the archbishop, and lived with him in Econe, makes this very claim (see Marcel Lefebvre: Sedevacanstist on YouTube by Rev. Anthony Cekada). Cekada's group of 9 priests left Econe because the archbishop refused to say publicly, what he was known to believe privately. Moreover, the very position of "recognize and resist" is an open admonition of schism. In the end, it really doesn't matter what an archbishop who died decades ago believed or didn't believe because Lefebvre was not infallible. To put the opinion of a bishop over the doctrines and dogmas of revealed truth would be to make Lefebvre on the same level of a True Pontiff, or even on the level of God Himself. In fact, the SSPX have become LeFebvrists and have not been able to lay claim to the title of Catholic for decades.

The second point above is even more outrageous. How can any person, much less those who call themselves Catholic, possibly believe that the almighty God, who created the universe and the Church itself, was impotent to bring a Head to His Church!? Rarely have I heard such blasphemy spoken by non-Catholics, but to hear it from a man in a cassock is uncommonly painful. There are many prophecies about a future pope being elected in an unusual manner. One such prophecy even says that "Saints Peter and Paul will descend from heaven to name the Pope." Why would we need such an unusual method of election if we still had the "usual means?"

The third point above is doctrinally ridiculous, and it is the line that many SSPX clergy feed their worried parishioners. This should not even have to be addressed, but I have found that so many people believe it that it begs an answer. One's biological father is defined by the person possessing an X and Y chromosome who gave one their DNA. A biological female (possessing 2 X chromosomes), cannot be a Father. She may have had an operation and may take hormones to grow a beard, and may dress like a man, but she is completely unable to donate the requisite sperm that fatherhood demands.

That's it.

To be the Pope of the Catholic Church there are two prerequisites: 1. He must be male (this one I am relatively certain that Bergoglio fulfils). 2. He must profess the Catholic Faith. This one isn't even close. Bergoglio's heresy is infamous, even in the Cult of the New Order. Yes, in the past we have had bad popes. But these men did indeed profess the Catholic Faith. They were just moral disasters, so they were dead members of the Church, but they were still members of the Church.

I have been told that forty years ago, during the reign of Karol Wojtyla (aka Antipole John Paul II), the SSPX clergy would say, "Everything the Pope (sic) writes, says or does, can be taken both in the light of tradition, or of modernism. If he were ever to teach anything clearly heretical, then he would lose his office, but he would drop dead before God would allow that to happen." This reasoning was false then because Wojtyla had already committed so many acts of heresy as to render this "line in the sand" crossed hundreds of times. And his heresies were evident before his supposed election, which would make him ineligible to lead the Church. And the "Church" to which he was elected ceased to be the Catholic Church when it adopted a host of new, invalid, and heretical sacraments. Fast forward to 2023, and the SSPX clergy no longer make this straw man argument as it is beyond any small shadow of a doubt that Jorge Bergoglio (aka Antipope Francis) is anything but a raging heretic. Even the SSPX clergy will openly admit he is. So, once again, the proverbial goal posts are moved, and the "if he would ever do x, y, z, then he would be a heretic" has been crossed over and over again, just to be ignored. With the latest from the arch-heretic, namely that homosexual "relationships" must be blessed by New Order clergy, the SSPX is once again condemning this action, but not coming to the obvious conclusion that the person who promotes such a heretical abomination cannot simultaneously be the leader of the Catholic Church.

And what about the SSPX sacraments? When offered by a man with valid traditional orders, the mass and sacraments must be assumed to be valid, but are they licit? Can an organization with such obvious schismatic internal logic give grace? I for one do admit that my family has received a great amount of grace from SSPX sacraments over the years. As the SSPX has not been formally named by a legitimate authority to be avoided, then canon law *appears* to allow for the faithful to avail themselves of these graces. Schismatics themselves may not receive grace from any sacraments:

> ***Cantate Domino (1441):*** *"The most Holy Roman Church firmly believes, professes and preaches that none of those people existing outside the Catholic Church, not only pagans, but also Jews and heretics and* **schismatics,** *can have a share in life eternal; but that they will go into the "eternal fire which was prepared for the devil and his angels" (Matthew 25:41), unless before death they are joined with Her;* **and that so important is the unity of this ecclesiastical body that only those remaining within this unity can profit by the sacraments of the Church unto salvation, and they alone can receive an eternal recompense for their fasts, their almsgivings, their other works of Christian piety and the duties of a Christian soldier.** *No one, let his almsgiving be*

*as great as it may, no one, even if he pour out
his blood for the Name of Christ, can be
saved, unless he remain within the bosom and
the unity of the Catholic Church."*

It goes without saying that when the Great Apostasy was
in its infancy, the confusion of the situation left many
innocent faithful Catholics floating in a sea of uncertainty.
But now, by the Grace of Almighty God, the Cult of the
New Order and its demonic leader (aka Francis) are so
obvious in their heresy, that no one with an average IQ
could possibly claim confusion. Those SSPX clerics who
persist in uniting themselves with this anti-Christ Bergoglio,
and those laity who insist on recognizing the Cult of the
New Order to be Catholic are now not only schismatic, but
also heretics.

    We have a direct correlation in the Life or Our Lord in
St. Luke's Gospel.

*Luke 8:43 And there was a certain woman having an
issue of blood twelve years, who had bestowed all her
substance on physicians, and could not be healed by
any. She came behind him, and touched the hem of
his garment; and immediately the issue of her blood
stopped. And Jesus said: Who is it that touched me?
And all denying, Peter and they that were with him
said: Master, the multitudes throng and press thee,*

and dost thou say, Who touched me? And Jesus said: Somebody hath touched me; for I know that virtue is gone out from me. And the woman seeing that she was not hid, came trembling, and fell down before his feet, and declared before all the people for what cause she had touched him, and how she was immediately healed. But he said to her: Daughter, thy faith hath made thee whole; go thy way in peace.

Hundreds, or maybe even thousands, of people surrounded Jesus, yet his grace was transmitted to just one faithful woman. Could it be that only faithful (Sedevacantist) Catholics are able to receive grace from SSPX sacraments? It would appear so. On the contrary, it is an article of Faith that schismatics do not receive grace from their sacraments. Let this knowledge strike fear into the SSPX clergy and laity who refuse to let their own common-sense reign.

Faithful Catholics must be careful if they do receive sacraments from SSPX clergy to confirm that the particular priest was, indeed, ordained from a LeFebvre line bishop. This is because in recent years the SSPX have taken in men ordained in the New Order, and sometimes have not re-ordained them in the Catholic Rite. It can be difficult to get a straight answer from the SSPX staff on this subject, which is suspicious at best and duplicitous as worst. The second pitfall to avoid is scandal. It is imperative that the faithful

Catholic does not try to "blend in" with the schismatics and that he/she should not hesitate to defend the truth that a heretic cannot be the leader of the Catholic Church. My own family never shrunk from this subject and made it quite known to all (including the priests) where we stood on this issue. To their credit, the priests never forbade us from receiving sacraments, but others have not been so fortunate. If a particular priest announces that he refuses to give sacraments to Sede-vacantists, then the faithful Catholic cannot attend individual priests' sacraments as it is then assumed by all that everyone in the church is schismatic and your very presence is a scandal to others.

"But", you ask, "where then would we receive the sacraments? I have heard that the Thuc line priests are not legitimate." This insidious rumour started decades ago. The facts of the situation have for the most part, quashed it, but there are some people who "didn't get the memo." I believe the best answer to the Thuc line issue can be found in a video by Father Francis Miller, who knew Archbishop Thuc well. In a nutshell, Thuc was lucid, and was quite brilliant. He knew exactly what he was doing and in the end was kidnapped by the New Order. His last words to the Faithful were of staunch determination to remain Catholic and to fight the New Order madness. It is a bit ironic, that if anyone were going to have dubious religious orders, it would be Archbishop Lefebvre as Cardinal Leinart who ordained him a priest was a rather infamous Freemason. As we do not have any admission by Leinart, we must, however, assume proper intention. Casting doubt on Archbishop Thuc, is a case of people unwittingly living in a glass house, yet throwing stones. In sum, if there is no danger of scandal, and there is no Sede-vacantist mass near, then the Faithful can avail themselves of the SSPX sacraments (at least until we have a true Pope who demands otherwise).

Much of today's confusion comes from the *name* Catholic. In fact, there are many non-Catholic sects who use the name Catholic. There is the Anglican Catholic Church and the Old Catholic Church for example. Catholic simply means "universal" and everyone wants to believe that their apostate group is part of the "Universal Body of Christ." Once we get it into our heads that the sect that was created from Vatican Council II is a completely different religion, with its own unique faith, sacraments, vestments, culture and hierarchy, and that it is in no way the same as the Catholic Church founded by Christ, the task of discerning the truth becomes much easier.

In the early 1970s, my great grandmother had just moved into the city from a little town in the woods of Minnesota. She had never been to a New Order service and was not even aware that there was such a thing. The first Sunday that she brought her twelve children to mass in their new neighborhood, she was bewildered by what she saw. Where was the altar? What were these strange vestments?

Why was the priest facing the people? She bent over to her youngest child who was eight years old at the time and said, "Geraldine, quick run and look at the sign outside. I think we are in the wrong church!" Geraldine came back and assured her mother that the sign said "Catholic", and so my great grandmother sat in the pew through the service and didn't question a thing.

In fact, the name "Catholic" will not save anyone, no more than the empty traditions of the Pharisees would save them. It is the true *Catholic Faith* that saves, and not the name. The New Order Cult is not Catholic, no matter what the sign says, and the sooner we start calling it by its proper name (New Order, or Novus Ordo Cult), the sooner we will all be able to get those of good will to exit the abominable Whore of Babylon.

Over the years my mother has "tried to talk sense" into many of her SSPX friends. My own Godmother is the mother of two SSPX priests and my Godfather is, himself, an SSPX priest. I write this out of my duty to them, as their Godson. I write this as a "wake up call" to the clergy and laity of the SSPX. The rituals and beauty of the Catholic sacraments are useless without the Faith. Remember Our Lord's admonition, "Your traditions will not save you!" A Spanish (Faithful Catholic) priest was once asked how to convince a "recognize and resister" that Francis cannot be the Pope of the Catholic Church. His answer was, "How do you convince someone that it is daytime? You take them outside and show them. If they refuse to admit the obvious, then there is nothing more to do." The sun rose decades ago on this issue. At this point, those who refuse to see the daylight are in danger of, or have already been, sent an "operation of error." We know that Our Lord warned us:

> *2 Thes. 2:10 And in all seduction of iniquity to them that perish: because they receive not the love of the truth, that they might be saved. Therefore God shall send them the operation of error, to believe lying: That all may be judged who have not believed the truth but have consented to iniquity.*

Dear SSPX friend, wake up! Your very soul is in peril. You can't have "your cake and eat it too." As you have united yourself with the leader of the Satanic Cult of the New Order in your very mass, you cannot also be a member of the Catholic Church. MAKE UP YOUR MIND.

Filling Up the Measure of the Elect

This first passage is read each year on November 1st, the Feast of All Saints.

God's People will Be Preserved

> *After these things, I saw four angels standing on the four corners of the earth, holding the four winds of the earth, that they should not blow upon the earth, nor*

upon the sea, nor on any tree. And I saw another angel ascending from the rising of the sun, having the sign of the living God; and he cried with a loud voice to the four angels, to whom it was given to hurt the earth and the sea, Saying: Hurt not the earth, nor the sea, nor the trees, till we sign the servants of our God in their foreheads. 144,000 Sealed And I heard the number of them that were signed, an hundred forty-four thousand were signed, of every tribe of the children of Israel.

Of the tribe of Juda, were twelve thousand signed: Of the tribe of Ruben, twelve thousand signed: Of the tribe of Gad, twelve thousand signed: Of the tribe of Aser, twelve thousand signed: Of the tribe of Nephthali, twelve thousand signed: Of the tribe of Manasses, twelve thousand signed: Of the tribe of Simeon, twelve thousand signed: Of the tribe of Levi, twelve thousand signed: Of the tribe of Issachar, twelve thousand signed: Of the tribe of Zabulon, twelve thousand signed: Of the tribe of Joseph, twelve thousand signed: Of the tribe of Benjamin, twelve thousand signed.

Praise from the Great Multitude. After this I saw a great multitude, which no man could number, of all nations, and tribes, and peoples, and tongues, standing before the throne, and in sight of the Lamb, clothed with white robes, and palms in their hands: And they cried with a loud voice, saying: Salvation to our God, who sitteth upon the throne, and to the Lamb. And all the angels stood round about the throne, and the ancients, and the four living creatures; and they fell down before the throne upon their faces, and adored

God, Saying: Amen. Benediction, and glory, and wisdom, and thanksgiving, honour, and power, and strength to our God for ever and ever. Amen. And one of the ancients answered, and said to me: These that are clothed in white robes, who are they? and whence came they? And I said to him: My Lord, thou knowest. And he said to me: These are they who are come out of great tribulation, and have washed their robes, and have made them white in the blood of the Lamb. Therefore they are before the throne of God, and they serve him day and night in his temple: and he, that sitteth on the throne, shall dwell over them. They shall no more hunger nor thirst, neither shall the sun fall on them, nor any heat. For the Lamb, which is in the midst of the throne, shall rule them, and shall lead them to the fountains of the waters of life, and God shall wipe away all tears from their eyes..

After the Elect Are Sealed and Protected

The Seventh Seal

Ordo Angelorum Daily Prayer to Saint Michael

Pope Leo XIII saw that the enemy would attack the See of Peter. This came to fruition with the takeover of the Vatican by the non-Catholic Sect of the New Order (Novus Ordo) and their installing an heretical anti-pope onto the throne.

By the Grace of Almighty God, this diabolical plan has now become so obvious with the heretical and Luciferian false faith of Jorge Bergolio (AKA, "Pope" Francis), that those who are truly seeking Truth can recognize the serpent and the serpent's false religion being presented to the world as Catholic.

This exorcism prayer is so powerful that Arch Heretic and Anti-pope Joseph Ratzinger (AKA "Pope Benedict XVI") forbade any lay people from reciting it, and even precluded priests and bishops who had not the training of an exorcist. Satan must be well aware of the efficacy of this prayer to want to squash it so completely.

We unite with all of the people of good will around the world to implore St. Michael and the angels to cast away all wickedness from God's Holy Church, to guide the elect to the One True Catholic Faith, outside of which no one is saved, and to protect the faithful in the times to come..

English

O glorious Archangel St. Michael, Prince of the heavenly host, defend us in battle, and in the struggle which is ours against the principalities and Powers, against the rulers of this world of darkness, against spirits of evil in high places (Eph 6:12). Come to the aid of men, whom God created immortal, made in his own image and likeness, and redeemed at a great price from the tyranny of the devil (Wisdom 2:23–24, 1 Cor 6:20). Fight this day the battle of the Lord, together with the holy angels, as already thou hast fought the leader of the proud angels, Lucifer, and his apostate host, who were powerless to resist thee, nor was there a place for them any longer in Heaven. But that cruel, that ancient serpent, who is called the devil or Satan, who seduces the whole world, was cast into the abyss with all his angels (Rev 12:7–9). Behold, this primeval enemy and slayer of man has taken courage, Transformed into an angel of light, he wanders about with all the multitude of wicked spirits, invading the earth in order to blot out the name of God and of his Christ, to seize upon, slay and cast into eternal perdition souls destined for the crown of eternal glory. This wicked dragon pours out, as a most impure flood, the venom of his malice on men of depraved mind and corrupt heart, the spirit of lying, of impiety, of blasphemy, and the pestilent breath of impurity, and of every vice and iniquity. These most crafty enemies have filled and inebriated with gall and bitterness the Church, the spouse of the Immaculate Lamb, and have laid impious hands on her most sacred possessions (Lam 3:15). In the Holy Place itself, where has been set up the See of the most blessed Peter and the Chair of Truth for the light of the world, they have raised the throne of their abominable impiety, with the iniquitous design that when the Pastor has been struck, the sheep may be scattered. Arise then, O invincible prince, bring help against the attacks of the lost spirits to the people of God, and bring them the victory. The Church venerates thee as protector and patron; in thee holy Church glories as her defense against the malicious powers of this world and of hell; to thee has God entrusted the souls of men to be established in heavenly beatitude. Oh, pray to the God of peace that He may put Satan under our feet, so far conquered that he may no longer be able to hold men in captivity and harm the Church. Offer our prayers in the sight of the Most High, so that they may quickly conciliate the mercies of the Lord; and beating down the dragon, the ancient serpent, who is the devil and Satan, do thou again make him captive in the abyss, that he may no longer seduce the nations. Amen.

Latin

Princeps gloriosissime caelestis militiae, sancte Michael Archangele, defende nos in proelio et colluctatione, quae nobis adversus principes et potestates, adversus mundi rectores tenebrarum harum, contra spiritualia nequitiae, in caelestibus. Veni in auxilium hominum, quos Deus creavit inexterminabiles, et ad imaginem similitudinis suae fecit, et a tyrannide diaboli emit pretio magno. Proeliare hodie cum beatorum Angelorum exercitu proelia Domini, sicut pugnasti contra ducem superbiae Luciferum, et angelos eius apostaticos: et non valuerunt, neque locus inventus est eorum amplius in coelo.Sed proiectus est draco ille magnus, serpens antiquus, qui vocatur diabolus et satanas, qui seducit universum orbem; et proiectus est in terram, et angeli eius cum illo missi sunt. En antiquus inimicus et homicida vehementer erectus est. Transfiguratus in angelum lucis, cum tota malignorum spirituum caterva late circuit et invadit terram, ut in ea deleat nomen Dei et Christi eius, animasque ad aeternae gloriae coronam destinatas furetur, mactet ac perdat in sempiternum interitum. Virus nequitiae suae, tamquam flumen immundissimum, draco maleficus transfundit in homines depravatos mente et corruptos corde; spiritum mendacii, impietatis et blasphemiae; halitumque mortiferum luxuriae, vitiorum omnium et iniquitatum. Ecclesiam, Agni immaculati sponsam, faverrimi hostes repleverunt amaritudinibus, inebriarunt absinthio; ad omnia desiderabilia eius impias miserunt manus. Ubi sedes beatissimi Petri et Cathedra veritatis ad lucem gentium constituta est, ibi thronum posuerunt abominationis et impietatis suae; ut percusso Pastore, et gregem disperdere valeant. Adesto itaque, Dux invictissime, populo Dei contra irrumpentes spirituales nequitias, et fac victoriam. Te custodem et patronum sancta veneratur Ecclesia; te gloriatur defensore adversus terrestrium et infernorum nefarias potestates; tibi tradidit Dominus animas redemptorum in superna felicitate locandas. Deprecare Deum pacis, ut conterat satanam sub pedibus nostris, ne ultra valeat captivos tenere homines, et Ecclesiae nocere. Offer nostras preces in conspectu Altissimi, ut cito anticipent nos misericordiae Domini, et apprehendas draconem, serpentem antiquum, qui est diabolus et satanas, ac ligatum mittas in abyssum, ut non seducat amplius gentes.O glorious Archangel St. Michael, Prince of the heavenly host, defend us in battle, and in the struggle which is ours against the principalities and Powers, against the rulers of this world of darkness, against spirits of evil in high places (Eph 6:12).

The Short Version Prayer

This short version Saint Michael exorcism was promulgated in 1902. For those who do not have time to recite the entire prayer, please take a few moments to pray this shortened one.

English

St. Michael the Archangel, illustrious leader of the heavenly army, defend us in the battle against principalities and powers, against the rulers of the world of darkness and the spirit of wickedness in high places. Come to the rescue of mankind, whom God has made in His own image and likeness, and purchased from Satan's tyranny at so great a price. Holy Church venerates you as her patron and guardian. The Lord has entrusted to you the task of leading the souls of the redeemed to heavenly blessedness. Entreat the Lord of peace to cast Satan down under our feet, so as to keep him from further holding man captive and doing harm to the Church. Carry our prayers up to God's throne, that the mercy of the Lord may quickly come and lay hold of the beast, the serpent of old, Satan and his demons, casting him in chains into the abyss, so that he can no longer seduce the nations.

Latin

Amen.Princeps gloriosissime caelestis militiae, sancte Michael Archangele, defende nos in proelio adversus principes et potestates, adversus mundi rectores tenebrarum harum, contra spiritalia nequitiae, in caelestibus. Veni in auxilium hominum, quos Deus ad imaginem similitudinis suae fecit, et a tyrannide diaboli emit pretio magno. Te custodem et patronum sancta veneratur Ecclesia; tibi tradidit Dominus animas redemptorum in superna felicitate locandas. Deprecare Deum pacis, ut conterat Satanam sub pedibus nostris, ne ultra valeat captivos tenere homines, et Ecclesiae nocere. Offer nostras preces in conspectu Altissimi, ut cito anticipent nos misericordiae Domini, et apprehendas draconem, serpentem antiquum, qui est diabolus et Satanas, et ligatum mittas in abyssum, ut non seducat amplius gentes. Amen

Ordo Angelorum Society

For more information on common errors and heresies held by those who consider themselves to be Christian see

FreedByTruth.org

GatheredSheep.org

Made in the USA
Las Vegas, NV
30 January 2024

84875200R00022